KU-203-781

Section 1. Foreword

As providers of services and as organisations working with staff, learners and partners from Black, Asian and Minority Ethnic groups (BAME) we are strongly committed to promoting equality of opportunity, and challenging discriminatory practices. The extent of cultural diversity within British society and the projected future demographic changes justifies such actions.

A number of organisations have recently been supported by the Department for Communities and Local Government (DCLG) through the Tackling Race Inequalities Fund (TRIF). Many of these have developed pioneering projects, and many have an exemplary track record of working in partnership, taking positive action and effecting change. The Network for Black Professionals (NBP), through it's Black Leadership Initiative (BLI®), is such an organisation.

The Good Practice Guide sets the equality standards all forward thinking and progressive organisations should be trying to achieve. It clearly demonstrates what works, in terms of race equality, the impact that good initiatives can have on the lives of people from BAME Backgrounds and the dedication and commitment of the many talented people who are engaged in highly effective work all over the country and on a daily basis.

The Good Practice Guide identifies the key elements necessary for success and how organisations might take these, tailor them and apply them to the work that they are doing with people from BAME groups. The guide highlights challenges faced by BAME organizations and how these can be overcome through working strategically and through partnerships.

The challenge is to turn the words in the guide into action and to make sure that the lives and opportunities of BAME citizens are improved at a local level. The NBP and the BLI® can support in this process through the dissemination of the guide, through stimulating discussion, and through giving practical advice and check lists which can support practitioners in developing their intercultural competencies.

Ultimately, this is about how organisations can ensure that they provide services which support people in maximizing their potential in education and in employment and in so doing, help to reduce inequalities.

Lord Herman Ouseley
February 2011

Class No.	305.	800941
Site	A9	181008
Processed by	SF	
Approved by	ENB	

NBP

About the Guide

In March 2009, the Department for Communities and Local Government announced £11 million available for two years to support organisations working in the area of race equality. The aim behind the Tackling Race Inequalities Fund [TRIF] was to help organisations promoting equality of opportunities, reducing inequalities, increasing civic participation by people from BAME backgrounds, and building their own capacity to do this work. This Guide has been commissioned by the NBP, as part of its TRIF activities, in order to share the BLI® model of good practice and some of the outcomes of that pioneering initiative.

Who is the Guide for?

The Guide is intended as practical help for senior managers and practitioners working in public and private organisations committed to improving their services for people from Black, Asian and Minority Ethnic groups. The Guide describes some of the practical approaches developed by the BLI® in order to improve an organisation's intercultural effectiveness. It also uses case studies to illustrate intercultural competencies in action by organisations with personal testimonials from people with BAME backgrounds. The case studies range from work with BAME people with learning disabilities to using football as a tool to promote community cohesion, and improving take-up of apprenticeships by BAME groups.

Using the Guide

Managers and practitioners can use practical approaches in the Guide to:

- understand more about intercultural competence and National Occupational Standards for intercultural working
- assess their organisation's intercultural effectiveness, and help staff to assess their readiness for working alongside staff from other cultures
- action plan to improve their organisation's effectiveness
- find out what other organisations are doing in their work with BAME groups
- find out about networks of organisations committed to improving services for BAME groups

Section 2.

Tackling Race Inequalities Fund

As well as providing funding through TRIF, the Department for Communities and Local Government was committed to help organisations play a more effective part in the development of equalities policy.

The initiative was part of a broader government commitment to equality demonstrated, for example, in the Communities and Local Government Department's Single Equality Scheme[1] which describes its responsibilities in creating communities which accept and value diversity as a source of strength and renewal, and, importantly, by the Equalities at Work Act. The Act came into force in October 2010; it draws together nine pieces of legislation, including those relating to race, religion, and belief, and makes it illegal to 'discriminate, harass or victimise another person because they belong to a group the Act protects'.

[1]Communities and Local Government's Single Equity Scheme, 2010-2013, DCLG, March 2010.

The TRIF monies were linked to six main TRIF themes:

1. promote equality of opportunity for people from Black, Asian and Minority Ethnic groups [BAME]

2. address inequalities of access and reduce gaps in outcomes for BAME people in a range of services, including education, health, housing, employment, and the justice system

3. undertake research into race equalities issues in order to increase the evidence base of the challenges facing BAME communities and how to tackle them

4. increase levels of civic participation, volunteering, or representation in civic or political institutions amongst BAME people

5. work with local bodies promoting race equality to help them work more effectively, including supporting the victims of racially-motivated crime

6. work with particularly disadvantaged people within BAME groups, including women, young people, and people with disabilities

The themes fit well with the idea of 'the big society' being developed by the new coalition government because they emphasise the importance of active participation in communities, local responses to local needs, and tackling the causes of inequality.

Section 3.
The Network for Black Professionals (NBP)

Robin Landman OBE CEO NBP

Twenty-six projects received TRIF support, ranging from vital, small local projects, to ambitious regional and national activities.

The NBP was one of the successful national organisations tendering for funds. The Network brought its thinking on intercultural competencies, its strong national network, and its tried and tested development strategies to the initiative.

There is more about the Network's role in the case studies, but some important messages from its work need to be stated here.

1. The Network found that financial resources were not always the biggest determinant of an organisation's ability to innovate in race equality. Instead, it was the knowledge, understanding and commitment to cultural diversity and to supporting BAME staff which made the difference.

2. Issues and challenges faced by BAME staff were the same, whatever the size or nature of the organisation. The most effective organisations deployed the skills and experiences of these staff to the full, and created employment pathways and career opportunities for them.

3. Good practice was as evident in parts of the country where there was little cultural diversity as it was in regions rich in racial mix.

The TRIF work took place at a time of serious discussion of what it takes for the UK to be a 'fair society'. The next section looks at this idea and some of its implications for race equality.

The Black Leadership Initiative (BLI®)

The Network approach to TRIF was to tailor and reapply a process and suite of BLI® opportunities that we knew from experience worked well in improving the career opportunities and life chances of BAME beneficiaries and supported in the development of intercultural competencies for all involved, irrespective of ethnic background. This meant adapting the BLI® model of programmes to meet the needs of the new sectors.

The BLI® was established in 2002 following the publication of the report of the Commission for Black Staff in Further Education. Supported by the NBP, the Association of Colleges and other stakeholder organisations, its brief was clear: to introduce practical measures that would improve career development opportunities for BME tutors, business support staff and managers working in the sector.

The Black-led BLI® is now the Professional development and Training service of the NBP and is committed to working with sector partners to achieve lasting change in the equality and diversity profile of the sector. The BLI® and the NBP are increasingly working across the schools, housing, voluntary and community and local government sectors in order to support Black professionals to achieve their career potential.

Since its inception in 2002 the BLI® has made a significant impact and achieved culture change within the Further Education sector raising the number of Black, Asian and Minority Ethnic leaders. The BLI® has also helped both BAME and non-BAME staff to benefit significantly from mentoring, secondment, career development and work shadowing opportunities.

The BLI® has pioneered the inspection shadowing programme in partnership with Ofsted in FE and extended the model to the National College for Leadership of Schools and Children's Services.

It has helped to change the landscape of leadership of FE and schools by raising the profile of BAME staff and through its practical career development strategies.

The BLI® is a cutting edge organisation which has gained worldwide recognition through its programmes.

Rajinder Mann Executive Director BLI®

The BLI® brings aspiring leaders together in a supportive and self critical environment and facilitates secondments and shadows for BAME staff enabling them to develop the skills, knowledge and experience they need to apply for senior posts and promotional opportunities.

The BLI® provides additional ongoing support such as focus groups and forums for Mentors participating in formal and informal mentoring relationships. Career advancement resources are also provided with development opportunities such as tailor-made workshops in association with private sector recruitment companies.

Network Approach

Our approach to TRIF is built on the success of the BLI® model in FE and reflects our philosophy in general when tackling inequalities and promoting cultural diversity. This meant that we focused on how we might best improve outcomes for individuals, hence our focus on promoting equality of opportunity for people from Black, Asian and Minority Ethnic groups, as well as how we might work with organisations to ensure that they treated BAME staff fairly.

In practice this translated into the delivery of individual programmes such as our Career Development Workshops, and organisational programmes such as our Intercultural Competencies Workshops and modular courses.

Individual and Organisational Development

We were able to offer several programmes designed to support BAME colleagues in improving their career prospects, the BLI® Career Development Workshops proved to be one of our most popular programmes. Aimed at colleagues at a range of levels and from a good cross-section of organisations, these workshops proved to be a reminder to colleagues of the importance of being proactive in facing the future. Workshops were delivered in a relatively direct and hard hitting way forcing participants to look at their skills and to look at their options and to thoroughly examine what they needed to do in order to achieve their career ambitions.

We were very clear through the Network that this was the most appropriate approach given our experience through the BLI® which had shown us that those colleagues who waited to be recognised for their skills, talents and qualifications (and these were numerous in our beneficiaries) often waited for very long periods of time and were very rarely recognised. Our focus was on identifying strengths, building on these and in encouraging colleagues to be proactive in carving out their own career path.

Our BLI® Career Development Workshops (CDWs) were all over subscribed; in fact we had to put on additional workshops, providing opportunities for approximately 100 colleagues. This course was rated by 100% of participants as being either good or excellent with the largest majority of participants marking it as excellent. The value of the BLI® CDWs was illustrated further through our Thematic Reviews and through the work carried out by the Change Institute. CDWs were identified as one of the single most important motivating factors giving TRIF participants the impetus to apply for new jobs, take advantage of promotion and enroll on work related training courses. All with a view of getting ahead of the competition and making oneself as marketable as possible.

Section 4.
A Fair Society?

In his speech to the Tory Party Conference on 6 October 2010, David Cameron set out his vision of a more powerful people in a fairer country. He said that the 'state of our nation is not just determined by government… but by what each of us do and what we choose not to do'. He wanted to ensure that 'everyone feels they belong' with 'a life fulfilled and fulfilling for everyone'. A vital part of achieving that vision was a power shift to local communities and local organisations 'from state power to people power'.

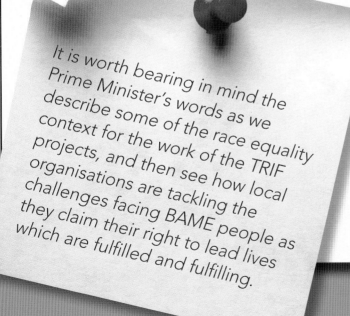

It is worth bearing in mind the Prime Minister's words as we describe some of the race equality context for the work of the TRIF projects, and then see how local organisations are tackling the challenges facing BAME people as they claim their right to lead lives which are fulfilled and fulfilling.

> **The recent report, 'How Fair is Britain?' from the Equality and Human Rights Commission provides some hard facts to set against the Prime Minister's vision.**

The Commission's first three year review of all aspects of equality, found in relation to race equality that:

- New challenges are emerging as the population ages and becomes more ethnically & religiously diverse

- Black Caribbean boys perform least well at GCSE-level

- Being Black and male has a greater impact on literacy level than even learning disability

- Black Caribbean and Chinese babies are twice as likely to die in their first year than White babies

- By age 22-24, some 44% of Black people are not in employment, education or training, compared to 25% of White people

- Five times more Black people than White people are in prison

- Pakistani, Bangladeshi, Black African Christian and Chinese men earn anything between 11% and 21% less than the average

- Only 47% of Muslim men are employed

Section 1
Section 2
Section 3
Section 4
Section 5
Section 6
Section 7
Section 8

The report describes five gateways to opportunity: well-being, education, work, security, and voice in society, but says that no matter how hard some people try, these gateways remain closed to them.

Some things have changed for the better: the Commission says Britain is more tolerant and open-minded, noting, for example, a significant drop in opposition to mixed-race marriages or to working for a BAME manager. For most BAME people, though, there is still a long way to go before they can achieve the equality which is the key to the fair society described by David Cameron.

Another smaller recent report adds to this picture of a still racially unequal society. According to The-Latest.com citizen journalism website, many local authorities still employ predominantly White people at senior levels even when their communities are mainly BAME. In London, for example, with 31% of the population from BAME backgrounds, only one council, Lambeth, has a Black chief executive.

The NBP's own research conducted by the Change Institute, begins its detailed and valuable report by describing some of the inequalities facing BAME people, whilst at the same time highlighting the emergence of a growing Black and Asian middle class and the high educational achievement of some ethnic minority groups. However, the report says differences in employment outcomes for BAME people and White people persist despite legislative changes. BAME people also face discrimination in relation to promotion and career progression, and in their representation at senior levels. The report continues by describing examples of positive action, for example, in the civil service, the police, and arts and culture sector, and provides examples of individual stories of success. Some of these personal testimonials can be found in shortened form as part of the Guide.

All this research, together with the living examples from the Tackling Race Inequalities Fund initiative show, as Trevor Phillips, Chairman of the Equality and Human Rights Commission says, 'We are people who have moved light years in our attitudes to all kinds of human difference, but … we are still a country where our achievements haven't yet caught up with our aspirations'.

The next part of the Guide introduces the idea of intercultural competence and the National Standards for Intercultural Working – approaches which will help Britain become a fairer society.

Section 5.

Intercultural competencies, National Occupational Standards, and self-assessment

By 2013, there is likely to be some 50% of new entrants to the labour market from BAME backgrounds.[2] Employers need the capacity to make best use of the new skills and perspectives that these people will bring to the workplace.

By 2016, there is likely to be a 47% increase in migration into the UK,[3] bringing new consumers and service-users who will want goods and services designed and delivered in ways that match their needs and aspirations. The links between these two facts is clear. Organisations able to deliver in the right way, as the NBP's research indicates, are those that have the right understanding of what BAME groups want. They will get this understanding from their own BAME staff.

Throughout its work programme, the Network emphasises the business case for race equality: do organisations, including those in the third sector, know enough about BAME groups to design and deliver what they need? Do they have enough BAME staff, including senior post-holders, to help them shape what they do effectively? Are they ready for the challenge?

The Network uses two instruments to assist organisations to think about their capacity and readiness. The instruments are the concept of Intercultural competencies and the National Occupational Standards for Intercultural Working.[4] As well as these two instruments, the Network developed practical self-assessment checklists which might be used by any organisation in any sector to check its capacity or readiness to meet the business challenges and opportunities provided by our country's changing racial profile.

[2] Office for National Statistics.

[3] Office for National Statistics.

[4] National Occupational Standards for Intercultural Working, The National Centre for Languages, 2008.

Section 5

Intercultural competencies

A working definition of intercultural competency is:

'Intercultural competence is the ability to communicate successfully with people of other cultures. A person who is interculturally competent captures and understands, in their interaction with people from foreign cultures, their specific concepts in perception, thinking, feeling and acting. Early experiences are considered, free from prejudices; there is interest and motivation to continue learning (about the person and their culture)'

Although this definition is about individual intercultural competence, it helps us think about an organisation's intercultural competence, because it makes clear that understanding, communication, and motivation to explore the relationship are at the heart of effective work with BAME groups.

In its TRIF and other activities, The NBP used the definition as a starting point in its work with organisations. The big questions are: 'What do intercultural competencies look like in practice? How do I know my organisation has them?'

National Occupational Standards for Intercultural Working

The National Occupational Standards for Intercultural Working help an organisation to answer these two key questions. The National Occupational Standards, developed in 2008 by The National Centre for Languages, describe the six key standards to be met by people working in organisations aiming to be effective, with customers and service-users from different countries or diverse cultures. The standards set out what staff need to know, do, and understand in order to be interculturally competent.

The six National Occupational Standards for Intercultural Working:

1. Develop your skills to work effectively with people from different countries or diverse cultures

2. Build working relationships with people from different countries or diverse cultures

3. Appoint people from different countries or diverse cultures

4. Manage a multi-cultural team

5. Manage delivery of a service to people from different countries or diverse cultures

6. Develop new markets with different countries or diverse cultures

Although the NBP originated in the further education sector, the TRIF initiative enabled it to extend its work using the National Occupational Standards into local government, and the public and third sectors.

Section 5

Leading the way to race equality

The business benefits of using the National Occupational Standards

Unit 1 of the National Occupational Standards: Develop your skills to work effectively with people from different counties or diverse culture, begins by setting out the benefits of the Unit and the Standards as a whole.

They reinforce the business case for effective intercultural working:

- improved cohesive workforce relations between people from different countries and diverse cultures

- reduction in workplace racism and workplace stress and the wasted time, potential and assets resulting from it

- work produced by individuals and teams that meets or exceeds work requirements

- services delivered sensitively and appropriately to all users

- service-users satisfied with the service they have received

- strengthened diversity and equality policies and procedures

The National Occupational Standards, which are validated by the relevant Sector Skills Councils, are complemented by other Management and Leadership Standards and Business Enterprise Standards thereby making them applicable to private, public, and third-sector organisations. Organisations can use intercultural working standards as a vital addition to the standards which set out what effective staff and managers do in the workplace. The chart shows how the sets of standards fit together.

In its TRIF work the Network used the National Occupational Standards for Intercultural Working as a basis for the design of professional development. Other organisations might use them in a similar way.

Section 1
Section 2
Section 3
Section 4
Section 5
Section 6
Section 7
Section 8

Standards for working with people from different countries or diverse cultures

The Standards for Intercultural Working are shown in bold. The complementary units from other sets of standards are shown in italics.

Source: The National Centre for Languages

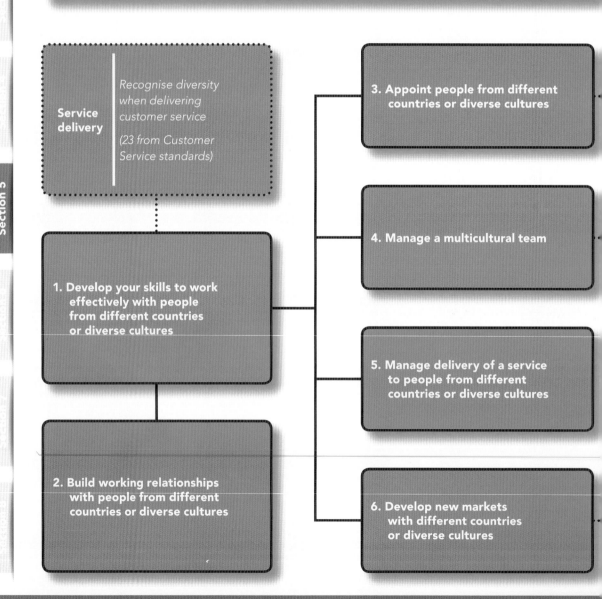

Service delivery

Recognise diversity when delivering customer service

(23 from Customer Service standards)

1. Develop your skills to work effectively with people from different countries or diverse cultures

2. Build working relationships with people from different countries or diverse cultures

3. Appoint people from different countries or diverse cultures

4. Manage a multicultural team

5. Manage delivery of a service to people from different countries or diverse cultures

6. Develop new markets with different countries or diverse cultures

Planning workforce requirements	*Plan what people the business needs (OP2 from Business Enterprise standards)*
	Plan the workforce (D4 from Management and Leadership standards)
Recruiting staff	*Recruit people (OP3 from Business Enterprise standards)*
	Recruit, select & keep colleagues (D3 from Management & Leadership standards)

Managing teams	*Make sure people can do their work (OP5 from Business Enterprise standards)*
	Allocate & check work in your team (D5 from Management & Leadership standards)
	Allocate and monitor the progress and quality of work in your area of responsibility (D6 from Management & Leadership standards)
Developing people	*Develop people's skills (OP6 from Business Enterprise standards)*
	Provide learning opportunities for colleagues (D7 from Management & Leadership standards)
Implementing workforce procedures	*Promote equality of opportunity and diversity in your area of responsibility (B11 from Management & Leadership standards)*
	Deal with workplace problems or disputes (OP7 from Business Enterprise standards)

Importing and Exporting	*Explore markets abroad (WB6 from Business Enterprise standards)*
	Import or export products or services (BD13 from Business Enterprise standards)

Section 1
Section 2
Section 3
Section 4
Section 5
Section 6
Section 7
Section 8

Self-assessment

As part of its TRIF activities, the NBP designed two self-assessment checklists so that organisations and individuals could explore the effectiveness of their own or their organisation's intercultural working.

Self-assessment checklist:

how effective is your organisation's intercultural working?

Read each statement and grade your organisation's response:

1 = we frequently do this. 2 = we occasionally do this. 3 = we rarely or never do this. Please feel free to photocopy this.

☐ My organisation's values, mission, policies, procedures and practices are reviewed regularly to ensure they promote effective intercultural working.

☐ My organisation's strategy, aims and objectives are informed by the experiences and needs of local BAME communities.

☐ My organisation sets performance targets relating to effective intercultural working.

☐ My organisation has development/ action plans which include activities to improve its intercultural working.

☐ My organisation systematically collects and uses data about customers'/service- users' cultural, linguistic and religious backgrounds and specific needs.

☐ My organisation evaluates regularly the ethnic mix of its customers/ service-users and compares it to the ethnic mix of the local population.

☐ My organisation uses the information it collects about the ethnicity of its customers/service-users to ensure its goods and services match what customers/service-users require.

☐ My organisation designs and delivers goods and services in partnership with BAME customers/service-users and their community representatives.

☐ My organisation has recruitment policies and practices which encourage the employment of people from BAME backgrounds.

☐ My organisation has a proportionate number of BAME staff at all levels, including senior roles.

☐ My organisation has measurable strategies to ensure BAME staff are retained, have career pathways and are promoted.

☐ My organisation provides professional development opportunities to enable staff to improve their intercultural working.

☐ My organisation has policies and practices which deter racial and ethnic slurs and harassment.

☐ My organisation encourages people from BAME backgrounds to participate in decision-making through its governing and management groups.

How did your organisation score?

Mainly 1s - Your organisation is well on the way to effective intercultural working. What could it do to maintain and develop its capacity?

Mainly 2s - Your organisation has some way to go before it is effective at intercultural working. The issue could be consistency across the organisation which may be effective in part. How might it build on its best practice to ensure 'top-to-toe' effectiveness?

Mainly 3s - Your organisation has challenges to tackle before it can be interculturally effective. How can it design an action plan to put it on the right road? How might it use local BAME community groups to help it?

The organisation's self-assessment should be used as part of its regular quality improvement and quality assurance processes. It has value as a 'one-off' exercise, but real change happens only when its outcomes are fed into the organisation's regular strategic and quality processes and plans. Intercultural working is not a 'bolt-on', but an integral part of what an organisation does and how it does it.

As part and parcel of the organisation self-assessment, organisations might wish to use an individual self-assessment with staff (see overleaf). The self-assessment looks at how 'ready' a staff member may be to work alongside staff from other racial or ethnic groups. Again, it is important that this activity is part of regular professional development with opportunities for staff to follow-through on their self-assessment outcomes by, for example, participation in structured training developed around the National Occupational Standards. Bear in mind that, although the 'readiness' of individual staff is an important aspect of an organisation's intercultural working, it is not all. Policies, processes and practices matter just as much. The individual self-assessment check-list was developed by the Network of Black Professionals.

The self-assessment helps staff think about their own readiness to work alongside staff from different racial or ethnic groups, as well as those with different cultural or religious backgrounds. Of course, its use is as relevant to staff with BAME backgrounds as it is for White staff.

Self-assessment checklist:

How ready are you for working alongside colleagues from different racial/ethnic backgrounds or from different cultures and religions?

Use the (A) boxes to place yourself where you think you are now. Use the (B) boxes to show where you would like to be.

Please feel free to photocopy this.

1. I enjoy working alongside people with different cultural experiences and perspectives from my own.

	Very like me	Like me	Not like me	A bit like me
A				
B				

2. I actively try to appreciate why differences and similarities may exist.

	Very like me	Like me	Not like me	A bit like me
A				
B				

3. I feel confident working alongside people with different cultural experiences and perspectives from my own.

	Very like me	Like me	Not like me	A bit like me
A				
B				

4. I am able to reflect on how my working practices may be perceived by others and am ready to negotiate new ways of working.

	Very like me	Like me	Not like me	A bit like me
A				
B				

5. I am open to how cultural diversity can improve ideas and working practices and effectiveness.

	Very like me	Like me	Not like me	A bit like me
A				
B				

6. I am sensitive to people's different levels of English language skills and am willing to adapt my language in the interests of mutual comprehension.

	Very like me	Like me	Not like me	A bit like me
A				
B				

7. I feel I have the skills to do this in a manner which helps mutual understanding.

	Very like me	Like me	Not like me	A bit like me
A				
B				

8. I am sensitive to how my use of language, tone of voice and behaviour may be interpreted by people from different racial, ethnic or cultural and religious backgrounds.

	Very like me	Like me	Not like me	A bit like me
A				
B				

9. I look critically at work practices and activities
    and make contributions designed to enhance
    intercultural cooperation and understanding.

	Very like me	Like me	Not like me	A bit like me
A				
B				

10. I believe I am working towards greater
    critical understanding of difference while
    appreciating that this is a lifelong process.

	Very like me	Like me	Not like me	A bit like me
A				
B				

11. I keep up-to-date with developments
    in equality and human rights, and take
    advantage of opportunities to improve
    my understanding and my practice.

	Very like me	Like me	Not like me	A bit like me
A				
B				

The self-assessment activity is best used as a starting point for reflection and discussion, and should lead to the identification of informal or formal professional development opportunities. Staff should not be 'left' with the outcomes with no follow-up opportunities.

Organisations may wish to add to or change the two self-assessment checklists to suit their own particular contexts.

Section 5

As well as using the National Occupational Standards and two self-assessment checklists, the Network of Black Professionals developed two sets of practical guidance for organisations working with BAME community groups and with BAME individuals. There are 'ten points to ponder' for each set of guidance. The first looks at what an organisation might need to think about in its work with BAME groups.

Ten points to ponder if your organisation is working with BAME groups

1. Do some research about the community groups you want to work with; find out about language, culture, religion, how established the community is, why people come to your area.

2. Establish contact with a representative who can act as an intermediary; people who represent the community or who know more about it than you can speed things up, and help you avoid any unnecessary pitfalls.

3. Review and reflect on your activities with community groups; there is always room for improvement.

4. Be clear about the purpose of your first contact; test your own expectations with the people you are meeting; are you offering something that people are going to value?

5. Develop case studies and exemplars to support your first contact or marketing activities; for some BAME groups, engagement with your organisation may involve a leap of faith; it helps if you can demonstrate that what you have to offer has worked well with other groups.

6. Use venues which are appropriate for the group(s) you want to work with; use your contacts and research to check suitability; check for significant religious or cultural days and avoid any clashes.

7. Make sure your work is mutually beneficial; agree a shared agenda; remember some of the groups you want to work with may have 'seen it all before', so be open about what you want to achieve.

8. Seek expert advice, but be aware that there may be different views within any community group; your organisation's capacity for intercultural working and its research into local community groups will be invaluable, particularly the skills and experience of your BAME staff.

9. Make sure you can guide people to other services; put together a database of other relevant organisations and use it to signpost people to sources of help, advice or other services.

10. Involve people from the community groups you want to work with; pay for specialist advice from community members; use the law to take positive action to appoint people from BAME groups who are under-represented in your organisation; this will show potential customers/ service-users that you are a good and knowledgeable employer, and add significant value to all your work including work with BAME groups.

Productive, well-informed engagement with local BAME groups encourages mutual respect and co-operation and leads to beneficial outcomes for everyone.

Section 1

Section 2

Section 3

Section 4

Section 5

Section 6

Section 7

Section 8

The second guidance suggests points for staff working with BAME adults. The guidance was developed in an education setting, but could be applied to work in any sector.

Ten points to ponder if you are working with customers/service-users from BAME backgrounds

1. Find out the basics about your customers'/service-users' culture, religion and tradition; watch what others in the group do, play safe if in doubt, for example it may not be acceptable for a man to shake a Muslim woman's hand.

2. Be aware that tensions may exist between different groups of people from the same country; for example, between people from Somalia and Rwanda.

3. Be aware of your own cultural values, and be prepared to be flexible in order to help customers/service-users feel comfortable.

4. Understand people's different expectations of your role; some cultures, for example, Chinese, may expect a more formal style of interaction than you might be used to.

5. Be aware of the impact on everyday life of religious traditions and festivals; for example, breaking the daily Ramadan fast at sunset means that people will wish to be at home by that time.

6. Resist stereotypical thinking; for example, Muslim people are not all the same – they may come from Arabic, African or European countries, be Black, Brown or White-skinned, and interpret the Quran conservatively or more liberally.

7. Be careful about the language you use to describe people; terms used to describe BAME people change all the time and some terms are not acceptable to everyone; preferences within one community can vary according to age, gender and social class.

8. Think about using mentors, volunteers, champions, coaches, work/study buddies and other high-profile role-models from BAME groups to help your BAME customers/service-users understand what they can achieve; invest in recruitment, training and support for these people; use positive action under the Race Relations Amendment Act to help make your staff more representative of the BAME groups you work with.

---

9. Foster close links with community organisations which act as bridges between your organisation and the BAME groups you want to work with; see the time you spend sustaining these relationships as an investment; make sure you acknowledge the contribution of these groups to your work.

---

10. Build on what you know about different cultures to develop new products and services which meet the needs of different BAME groups; your BAME colleagues' knowledge and understanding will be invaluable here, as well as your good relationships with community representatives.

These ten points to ponder could be used in conjunction with the self-assessment checklist designed to help individual staff to assess their readiness for working alongside colleagues from BAME backgrounds, and to help a staff team reflect on its own practices and to action-plan for improvement.

This section of the Guide has described some of the instruments used by the NBP in its TRIF activities across a variety of sectors. Together, the instruments offer real practical help to organisations and individual staff working with BAME groups. The next section looks at intercultural working in action through case studies contributed by various projects.

Section 5

Section 1

Section 2

Section 3

Section 4

Section 5

Section 6

Section 7

Section 6.
Case studies.

Leading the way: effective intercultural working in action

The case studies show effective intercultural working in action in organisations which are leading the way to race-equality. A commentary at the end of each case study analyses the things the organisation is doing which make it a leader. Organisations might find it useful to consider each case study in the light of The National Occupational Standards and the self-assessment checklist: how effective is your organisation's intercultural working?

NBP: extending work with other sectors.

The organisation

The NBP is a social justice, not-for-profit organisation founded in 1998 to tackle under-representation of Black staff in further education. Its work includes policy development, research, and practical assistance to individuals and organisations tackling race inequality. The training and developmental activities including mentoring support are delivered through the BLI®.

The challenge

The challenge for the Network was to extend the approaches it had developed in further education through the BLI® to other sectors, in particular working with strategic and senior managers in local government, the voluntary and community sector and in a range of public services.

Activities

As part of its TRIF activities, BLI®:

- held nine regional training and development events including mentor training, mentee induction, overview programmes for strategic and senior managers from local authorities and voluntary and community groups, and diversity in action workshops tailored to all sectors

- made some 60 presentations to conferences and other events to introduce the National Occupational Standards for intercultural working, the BLI®, and other successful approaches used by the Network

- ran best practice events to share ideas between TRIF project participants

- linked these activities to other Network activities, including work shadowing, career development workshops, master classes, thematic seminars, and its Talent Management Programme

- commissioned an important research report: Race Inequalities and Positive Action

- sponsored this Guide: Leading the Way

Case study 1 NBP: extending work with other sectors. CONTINUED...

Impact

Impact included:

- more organisations and services able to use the instruments and approaches developed by the Network, and the National Occupational Standards

- rigorous research which evidenced the value of Positive Action through large-scale case studies, thereby encouraging other organisations to adopt this strategy

- cross-fertilisation of ideas and practice between different sectors and organisations

- supportive forum which encouraged organisations to reflect on their intercultural working, and to plan to improve it

- knowledgeable, practical support for senior BAME staff, including an innovative BLI® mentoring scheme, which helped open career doors

- BAME staff better able to help inform and develop the intercultural working of their organisations

- organisations better able to assess their intercultural working, and to plan how to improve it through, for example, more effective recruitment of BAME staff, and better links with local BAME groups

- involvement of decision-makers such as chief executives and directors who are better placed to direct their organisations' intercultural strategies

- subsidised development opportunities for sectors, eg third sector, which are experiencing cuts

The Network found that though it was sometimes difficult for staff to find the time to attend events, particularly if they were from the hard-pressed third sector, demand for BLI® career development workshops and requests for mentors were higher than ever during this time of economic recession.

Leading the Way

The NBP is leading the way through its BLI® because:

- it is a Black-led organisation, using an effective mix of research and practical action to tackle race inequality by working with individuals and organisations

- it is able to help inform policy-making through its good links with government departments

- it has extended understanding and skills gained initially in one sector into other sectors

- it listens hard to what its BAME participants and members want and then delivers it

- it works productively and in partnership with other organisations tackling race inequality, helping them to build on what they already do

Case study 2

Liverpool JET Service: providing employability services to BAME groups

The organisation

Liverpool Jet Service works in partnership with Liverpool Adult Learning Services to deliver independent employment advice and guidance to BAME communities.

The challenge

The challenges for Liverpool Jet Service were to build relationships and trust with ethnic minority groups in the most deprived areas of Liverpool in order to help members take the first steps into employment.

Activities

As part of its TRIF activities, JET has:

- provided specialised support to local Congolese, Yemeni, Polish, Czech, and Kurdish communities

- put together key data on employment and language support needs of migrant workers to help inform important research by Liverpool University and Salford University

- worked with employers who are employing people whose first language is not English

- helped policy development through involvement with the Merseyside Refugee Support Network

- worked collaboratively with other local groups, including Women's Somali groups, Health Professional Refugee Network, and Community Women's Focus Group

Impact
Impact included:

- over two years, registering nearly 900 BAME people with the Service, thereby ensuring they received the specialist help they required

- progressing over 20% of these people into employment at a time of economic recession

- getting people into work at a lower cost than other schemes

- making sure people could 'convert' their qualifications to UK standards, making it easier for potential employers to understand their skills

Leading the Way
Liverpool JET Service is leading the way because:

- it consists of a small, effective team including multiple language speakers and staff from BAME backgrounds who understand the communities they work with

- it uses outreach working to take the Service to the communities

- it provides a holistic service, including ESOL training, discretionary grants and referrals to other services

Section 1
Section 2
Section 3
Section 4
Section 5
Section 6
Section 7
Section 8

Case study 3

Black Training and Enterprise Group: closing the Ethnic Minority Apprenticeship Gap in Yorkshire and The Humber

The organisation

BTEG is a national charity providing a voice to government for Black, Asian and Minority Ethnic (BAME) voluntary, community and social enterprise organisations. BTEG works in partnership with the National Apprenticeship Service (NAS) for Yorkshire and The Humber and the BME Learning Network, as well as local BAME groups and providers.

The challenge

BTEG's challenge was to raise awareness of poor representation of BAME young people on the region's Apprenticeship programmes, and to begin to scope the issues and how they might be tackled.

Activities

As part of its CLG Tackling Race Inequalities Fund activities, BTEG convened a conference for employers, providers and local authorities in partnership with NAS where it:

- used national and regional BAME employment data to make the case for increasing BAME representation in the Apprenticeship programme
- identified key questions including:
  - what key barriers in Yorkshire and The Humber affect participation in Apprenticeships by BAME groups?
  - how do we promote and raise awareness of Apprenticeships to potential BME Apprentices and amongst BAME employers?
  - how do we identify and share good practice in Yorkshire and The Humber?
  - are the key agencies focusing on the issue sufficiently (Job Centre Plus, Local Councils, Skills Funding Agency, NAS, Young People's Learning Agency)?
- linked these questions to the need for the systematic collection and analysis of data about BAME recruitment and retention in Apprenticeships
- used national DIUS research to demonstrate that BAME Apprentices are likely to be concentrated in low earning, low opportunity sectors
- used an inquiry by the National Skills Forum to show that BAME employers in small and medium enterprises are put off the Apprenticeship programme by its complicated funding and bureaucracy

Case study 3 Black Training and Enterprise Group: closing the Ethnic Minority Apprenticeship Gap in Yorkshire and The Humber CONTINUED...

Impact
Impact has included:

- 43 organisations taking part in group work sessions about closing the ethnic minority gap and providing solutions
- BTEG establishing new links with businesses and possibilities for developing examples of good practice
- examples of good practice from In communities Property Solutions in Bradford and Path Yorkshire made available on the website to BTEG's network of over 600 contacts
- BTEG sharing with NAS the key recommendations raised by conference participants
- BTEG hosting another over-subscribed Apprenticeship event with NAS in London on developing an equalities action plan for NAS
- young people receiving information and guidance about Apprenticeships through BTEG's Apprenticeship for ME project

Leading the way
BTEG is leading the way because:

- it influences policy development whilst providing organisational support for voluntary, community and social enterprise organisations
- as a member of the Department for Business Innovation and Skills Equality Advisory Group, it calls for NAS to take action on equality
- it promotes Apprenticeships to young people at schools and youth events through the Apprenticeships for BAME project
- it is delivering the national REACH role model programme and bursary scheme
- it has produced briefing papers and reports on under-representation of BAME people in Apprenticeships, and on employment, education and poverty
- it has established and developed BAME forums and networks

Section 1
Section 2
Section 3
Section 4
Section 5
Section 6
Section 7
Section 8

Case study 4
OLMEC: supporting a new social entrepreneur

The organisation

OLMEC's First Steps programme helps 'start up' social enterprises from BAME communities. The programme is interactive with individualised support for the entrepreneur, and realistic emphasis on establishing appropriate governance, legal structures, policies and processes to enable the business to compete for contracts.

The challenge

It is hard to begin any new business in a recession. The challenge tackled by the First Steps programme was to help individuals from BAME and refugee communities test out their business ideas and to find out what was needed to make them a reality.

Activities

As part of its TRIF activities, the First Steps programme worked with Jide Pitan who wanted to help BAME young people in London overcome barriers to success. First Step supported Jide by:

- providing a ten-day training programme and tailor-made individual support to help him clarify what his new organisation Nu-Breed Enterprises might offer young people, identify and understand the market, prepare a business plan, and register as a company

- offering help flexibly in ways and in venues that fitted with Jide's domestic and business commitments, including evening and weekend meetings

- taking account of his need to 'own' his enterprise whilst encouraging inclusive governance which involved a wider group of people with complementary skills

- helping Nu-Breed Enterprises select the legally right structures and governance

- assisting Jide to register his new organisation so it could tender for contracts

- assisting with policy development and a Community Interest Statement

- making further support available as the enterprise takes off, for example, help with strategies for growth and for marketing

Impact

Impact for this new entrepreneur included:

- clarity over what services Nu-Breed Enterprises would offer: sports activities, martial arts, information and advice

- understanding the steps he needed to take to turn his original vision into reality

- security of someone knowledgeable to turn to

- knowledge of start-up business processes and legal requirements

- structured help with business planning

- an effective business, able to secure a £50,000 contract to deliver information, support and advice to young people for Metropolitan Housing

- BAME young people are benefiting from the services he provides

Leading the Way

OLMEC's First Steps programme is leading the way because:

- it recognised that Jide had the potential to be an outstanding entrepreneur, and built on his knowledge of BAME young people developed in his earlier work as a martial arts instructor

- it provided structured, individualised support which took account of his circumstances

- it gave him the skills he needed to compete successfully for contracts

Case study 5
People First Merseyside: valuing all our communities

The organisation

People First is a long-established self-advocacy organisation of people with learning disabilities. In Merseyside, it works collaboratively with the Liverpool Learning Disability Making it Happen Partnership, and with Chara Trust and Legacy project. Liverpool City Council funded a part-time worker to assist with the TRIF work.

The challenge

BAME people with learning disabilities experience barriers in accessing advocacy services which could help them to specialist health and social services. For People First Merseyside, the challenge was to increase the number of BAME People First self-advocates and to use these new members to raise awareness of the issues facing BAME learning-disabled people as they try to access services.

Activities
As part of its TRIF activities, People First has:

- worked with BAME community organisations, including the Pakistan Centre, Al-Ghazali Multicultural Centre, Caribbean Centre, West African Elders, Kenyan Association, Chinese Carers Development Association and Irish Community Care to inform them of People First and to encourage membership from people with learning disabilities in these communities

- participated in training on intercultural competencies and on leadership provided by the NBP

- worked as 'experts by experience' to demonstrate to regional and local conferences some of the barriers faced by BAME people with learning disabilities, and how they overcome some of them by using Person Centred Planning and personalised budgets

- joined the Speak Out Network which represents different community groups wishing to find a voice, thereby making common cause with other under-represented groups; Speak Out is supported by the University of Central Lancashire

- ensured BAME people with learning disabilities took part in a Liverpool Citizen Advocacy Hub event

- ran workshops with BAME self-advocates at a regional conference run by Aim Higher, with representatives from unions and learning and skills sectors

Impact

Impact included:

- increase in the number of BAME self-advocates able to speak out for what they need from services

- better understanding of effective intercultural working by staff supporting the self-advocates

- new relationships with BAME communities which have not traditionally accessed services for people with learning disabilities

- increased understanding of the needs of BAME people with learning disabilities by People First and by service providers

- further invitations for People First BAME self-advocates to participate in regional and national conferences and meetings, including membership of the British Institute for Learning Disabilities National Advisory Group on Learning Disabilities and Ethnicity

- plan to recruit more staff from BAME communities

Leading the way

People First Merseyside is leading the way because:

- it empowers BAME people with learning disabilities to speak for themselves

- it enables these people to access the services they need

- it raises awareness of learning disabilities amongst BAME communities

- it builds on strong relationships with BAME representatives to work with groups which are traditionally hard to reach where disability is concerned

Path Yorkshire: pre-Apprenticeship programme

The organisation

Path Yorkshire is a charity set up originally by a local authority to promote Positive Action training in housing management. It now covers all areas of employment, working in partnership with the academic, business, statutory and voluntary sectors.

The challenge

The challenge for Path Yorkshire was to take practical Positive Action to encourage BAME young people into Apprenticeships, working in partnership with Connexions, Job Centre Plus, further education colleges, Leeds City Council and local businesses.

Activities

As part of its TRIF activities, Path Yorkshire has:

- designed a six-month pre-Apprenticeship programme for BAME young people interested in the Construction, Vehicles/Engineering, Catering and Hairdressing sectors
- identified BAME young people from deprived areas, and BAME and non-BAME small and medium employers
- marketed the programme through regional information and recruitment days, and by e-mail to 1500 BAME people on Path's and other community and voluntary organisations' databases
- set up work placements for 30 trainees
- supported trainees through the programme with dedicated support and close monitoring of progress against individual training plans
- included as part of the programme, a bespoke package to support personal development and employability skills, including units toward accreditation in Effective Thinking

Impact

Impact included:

- 30 BAME trainees able to enter the full Apprenticeship programme
- more BAME businesses involved in the programme
- raised awareness of the needs of potential BAME Apprentices amongst providers
- a model of preparation for Apprenticeships for use by other voluntary organisations and providers

Leading the way
Path Yorkshire is leading the way because:

- it is a well-established BAME organisation with a good record of successful Positive Action programmes

- its management committee members are from diverse backgrounds with extensive experience of training and of BAME young people

- it works effectively with key stakeholders

- it has the data and IT systems to track trainees and to monitor their progress, and to monitor its own effectiveness

- it is evaluating the programme and intends sharing what it has learned with other organisations

Section 6

Case study 7
The Rural Media Company: Travellers' Times magazine for Gypsies and Travellers

The organisation

The Rural Media Company is an award-winning education, production and development charity based in the West Midlands, with an emphasis on work with rural and disadvantaged communities.

The challenge

The challenge for the Rural Media Company was to provide a voice for Gypsy, Roma and Travelling (GRT) communities which combated the often stereotypical and racist coverage by the media. The Company's own research indicated that community members wanted to keep the print version of the magazine as well as the Travellers' Times website.

Activities

The Rural Media Company's TRIF activities included:

- recruiting a project co-ordinator and marketing officer for the magazine, both of whom are Travellers

- redesigning the Travellers' Times to make it accessible for people with low literacy levels

- including at least six items per issue which help promote equality and Gypsy, Roma and Travellers' achievements, as well as describing good practice in housing, health and civic participation

- establishing a new database of subscribers and enquiries and helping reduce overhead costs

- launching a new subscription scheme and increased advertising income

- planning for greater financial stability for the magazine which acts as a stepping stone to the website

Impact

Impact included:

- better bridges between Gypsy, Roma and Travelling communities and with the rest of society

- support for public and voluntary sector workers accessing GRT sites and communities

- raised positive awareness and understanding of GRT concerns and cultures

- positive models of GRT achievements

- training resource for organisations working with the communities, including schools, police forces, and social services

One traveller says:

'It has helped me learn that change can only come from those who want it … I have a voice that millions of people can hear. It has helped me to stand up for what I believe in which is educating people in our race, our culture, traditions, our lives … and this encourages other Travellers to become Gypsy liaison officers, or police officers, or nurses'.

Another traveller says:

'It is not just a magazine that keeps you up-to-date on planning, evictions, weddings and bereavements, it also encourages young Gypsy and Traveller people to be proud of their heritage, to seek employment, enter competitions, and to communicate with the settled community. It gives people a chance to be educated in a way of life that has continued for six hundred years'.

Leading the way

Travellers' Times is leading the way because:

- it employs people with strong roots in the communities it serves
- it rotates its editorial group meetings round the country so representative groups such as The Gypsy Council and the National Travellers Action Group are able to attend and are included in decision-making
- it records, celebrates and communicates what happens in marginalised parts of our society
- it combats prejudice and stereotyping by offering a positive picture of GRT communities

Section 6

Case study 8

The Roots Research Centre: the National BAME Youth Survey

The organisation

The Roots Research Centre works for and with BAME communities. In the TRIF initiative, it worked in partnership with the Centre for Local Policy Studies at Edge Hill University and with Equanomics UK.

The challenge

Unemployment amongst BAME young people is currently 34% compared to 21% for the overall age group. We need to know more about the experiences of these young people, and to understand more about the barriers they face.

Activities

As part of its TRIF activity, the Roots Research Centre:

- designed and managed a National BAME Youth Survey
- recruited five BAME young people who were not in education, employment or training to lead the Survey
- trained the young people in research methods
- supported these researchers in running focus groups of BAME young people
- helped identify the issues raised in the focus groups
- used junior staff to support the researchers so the Survey was genuinely led by young people
- disseminated the research findings to other third sector and statutory organisations

Leading the way

The Roots Research Centre is leading the way because:

- BAME young people led research which was about their peers
- the young researchers all moved on to paid employment, boosted by the training and opportunities they were given by leading the Survey

ROTA: Female Voice in Violence

The organisation

Race on the Agenda (ROTA) is an independent research and social policy charity based in London, which focuses on issues facing BAME communities. Its Female Voice in Violence project grew from ROTA's award-winning Building Bridges project which was a youth-led investigation into gangs and weapons-use in London.

The challenge

Inability to access services and support may contribute to the victimisation and isolation of BAME women experiencing violence. Specialist and generic support services need to know more about these women's experiences in order to respond more effectively.

Activities

As part of its TRIF activity for the Female Voice in Violence project, ROTA:

- designed and undertook field research led by BAME young people
- hold group interviews, round-tables and discussions with specialist services and women's organisations to explore the issues and find out more about service responses
- developed policy recommendations through work with five London boroughs culminating in a pan-London meeting hosted by the Greater London Authority, and a meeting with government department representatives hosted by the Government Equalities Office

Section 1
Section 2
Section 3
Section 4
Section 5
Section 6
Section 7
Section 8

Case study 9 ROTA: Female Voice in Violence. CONTINUED...

Impact
Impact included:

- a set of high-level recommendations designed to ensure that BAME women experiencing violence are taken fully into account in policy development and service design

- recommendations for changes in practice to combat youth violence

- recommended review of child protection strategies and guidance to include tackling violence against BAME women, including sexual violence

- increased awareness of the issues, including the lack of hard data about the numbers of women and girls affected by gang violence, and about practices which sometimes serve as barriers to BAME women and girls dealing with their victimisation

Leading the way
ROTA is leading the way because:

- its Female Voice in Violence provides a valuable voice for BAME women and girls who are usually silent about their experiences of violence

- the project helped voluntary and statutory services to assess the effectiveness of their response to the issue, and to improve what they do

- the work led to policy recommendations signed up to by government and local government

- it highlighted good practice in supporting women and girls in changing their lifestyle and escaping violence

Case study 10
Wirral Council Black Workers Group: Wirral United Trophy – Giving Discrimination the Boot

The organisation

The Black Workers Group from Wirral Council works locally to tackle race inequality. For the Giving Discrimination the Boot project, the Group worked with over eight statutory and voluntary services to demonstrate that different racial groups could act together to combat race-hate incidents.

The challenge

Race-hate incidents were taking place in Wirral where both victims and perpetrators were male. Merseyside Police and the BAME communities wanted an activity that could pull together different racial groups and provide opportunities for adults and children to learn more about race-hatred and how to combat it. Football was the answer!

Activities
The Black Workers Group's TRIF activities included:

- two football tournaments for primary and secondary school children, with trophies, medals, special pitches and professional referees

- stalls and activities such as Show Racism the Red Card which focused on dealing with race hatred and bullying, as well as on healthy lifestyles, free health checks, and health issues such as sickle-cell anaemia and thalassaemia

- using young volunteers to host the tournaments

- free tennis demonstrations by a professional coach at the tournaments

- entertainment from African drummers and hip-hop dancers, as well as workshops about African culture

- football freestyling workshops and demonstrations

- a Hall of Fame of BAME Merseyside footballers, to coincide with Black History Month

- free food donated by a local Indian restaurant

Section 1
Section 2
Section 3
Section 4
Section 5
Section 6
Section 7
Section 8

Case study 10 Wirral Council Black Workers Group: Wirral United Trophy – Giving Discrimination the Boot. CONTINUED...

Impact
Impact included:

- strengthened relationships between the eight partners, which included community groups, private football companies, statutory organisations, and the local council

- better awareness of race-hate crime and bullying and how to tackle them amongst children and the communities supporting the project

- increased understanding of how to access services such as the police

- a more cohesive and engaged community which knows it can work together

- new partnership between key representatives of the community and the council who worked collaboratively to deliver the project

- concrete plans to turn the tournaments into an annual event, supported by Tranmere Rovers and the same funders

- plans to affiliate with the Football Association League to enable teams to access pitches and other tournaments

Leading the way
The Black Workers Group and its partners are leading the way because:

- strong leadership from the Chair of the Group helped drive the project

- effective collaboration between a variety of groups and services meant footballers and their families had a great experience and learnt a lot about other races, as well as understanding more about race-hate crimes

- all the partners put money and time into the project, making a shared commitment to its success

- young volunteers and young referees enjoyed opportunities to develop skills in real-life situations

Oxfam: Routes to Solidarity

The organisation

Oxfam is an internationally respected third sector organisation operating abroad and in the UK. It wanted its race equality programme to be informed by the needs and demands of the UK's established and newly-emerging BAME communities. In its three-year Routes to Solidarity project, Oxfam worked with BAME women's organisations in the North West, Yorkshire and the Humber, and the North East.

The challenge

Women from BAME communities are significantly under-represented in public and political life. They face multiple discrimination because of their race and gender. Some 40% of BAME women live in poverty, compared to about 20% of the general population. The project's aim was to help the grass-roots organisations which represent these women to build on their existing expertise and to magnify their impact on policy and on individual women's lives.

Activities
**Oxfam's Routes to Solidarity
TRIF activities included:**

- adopting three systematic levels of working: influencing policy and decision-making, grass-roots training, organisational networking and lobbying

- influencing policy and decision-making involving policy round tables, briefing papers and submissions to government consultations, lobbying, and identifying examples and case studies from the partners

- grass-roots work involving training 120 women from 60 BAME organisations, with intensive support and coaching for some 20, and assistance with action-planning

- developing new regional networks, thirty lobbying activities, and eight new community cohesion projects, as well as regular newsletters of information and updates for partners and service providers

- plans to extend the project for two more years

Section 1
Section 2
Section 3
Section 4
Section 5
Section 6
Section 7
Section 8

Impact

Impact included:

- five new networks of BAME women's organisations in the North of England
- empowered BAME women's organisations more effective at making their voices heard and better able to influence policy-making
- common cause between organisations representing different racial groups
- BAME women with improved understanding of their rights and able to exercise leadership in economic, social and political spaces
- better informed policy-makers more able to design solutions that benefit BAME communities

Oxfam's Routes to Solidarity is leading the way because:

- it builds directly on the expertise and experience of small BAME community groups to influence policy
- it demonstrates the power of solidarity between different BAME groups with similar agendas
- it shows how a large NGO can work sensitively and skillfully to develop the capacity of small organisations, and to help inform its own policy and practice in the process

One participant at the Leeds-based training said:

'Routes to Solidarity has fired up little sparks that are burning inside of me; it has brought back the vibrancy in me'.

The BLI® and the NBP: practical support for individuals

The organisation

The BLI® and the NBP has been described earlier in the Guide. This case-study describes three of the TRIF supported activities it used with new sectors.

The challenge

CLG had cited the BLI® as a model of good practice in the education sector; the TRIF initiative enabled it to rethink and apply its well-established approaches in other sectors, including large services and small community-based organisations. This meant extending its activities and working with managers and staff in different kinds of organisations.

Activities

BLI's® TRIF activities included:

- residential mentor training for potential mentors, with an introduction to the GROW model of coaching, and opportunities to explore the practical aspects of being a mentor, as well as learning about the challenges faced by BAME staff and issues relating to cross-cultural mentoring

- mentee induction programme for junior BAME staff wanting to support and develop their careers, with practical information about the benefits of having a mentor and links to the BLI® mentoring programme

- its pioneering Diversity in Action course designed to help senior managers develop their intercultural competencies, using the National Occupational Standards and the checklists in this Guide

Impact

Impact included:

- organisations in other sectors being more knowledgeable about effective intercultural working

- cross-fertilisation of ideas and practice between the education sector and other sectors

- junior BAME staff able to join mentee scheme

- senior BAME staff encouraged to serve as mentors

Leading the way

The NBP is leading the way because:

- it understood the value and applicability of its approaches to other sectors and had the credibility and skills to adapt them for their use

- its activities help individuals and organisations become more effective at intercultural working

- it understands why BAME staff need to be at every level, including the most senior, in an organisation if it is to provide the goods and services BAME communities want, and it is able to provide the right assistance to help this happen

Case study 13
One North West:
NW BAME Policy Forum

The organisation

One North West is a regional Network working with BAME voluntary and community sector organisations in the North West in order to influence decisions which will lead to better outcomes for the communities they serve.

The challenge

The success of the coalition government's Big Society idea rests on the capacity of third sector organisations to take a bigger role in providing services and in advocating on behalf of their communities. If organisations work together they can learn from each other, and speak with a more unified voice, thereby becoming much more influential in policy formation.

Activities

One North West's TRIF activities included:

- providing a Policy Forum for BAME groups
- offering development opportunities and training in human rights, public law, and measuring impact
- supporting conversations about the role for BAME groups within the Big Society agenda
- joint work with Oxfam's TRIF-funded Routes to Solidarity leading to a BAME Women's Charter

Impact

Impact included:

- more unified voice for BAME groups in the North West
- 200 BAME groups better able to engage with national decision-making and to campaign for race equality
- 200 BAME groups with increased capacity to play an active part in the Big Society agenda
- increased trust between different BAME groups

Leading the way

One North West is leading the way because it:

- understood the opportunities and challenges of the Big Society agenda for BAME organisations
- brought together a diverse range of BAME organisations into a single coalition
- made it possible for organisations to be 'more than the sum of their parts' by helping them to learn from each other and to learn how to influence policy

Section 3

Section 2

Section 3

Section 4

Section 5

Section 6

Section 7

Section 8

Case study 14
Stephen Lawrence Charitable Trust: Bursary and Alumni Programme evaluation

The organisation
The Stephen Lawrence Charitable Trust was established in 1998 in order to make architecture and related professions accessible to disadvantaged young people. Part of its work is to award bursaries to BAME young people wishing to train as architects or to specialise in the built environment sector.

The challenge
Considerable research evidence indicates that barriers such as lack of financial support mean that less than 4% of registered architects come from BAME backgrounds. Other barriers include difficulty in accessing work placements, partial understanding of what the profession entails, limited networks of people able to provide the right professional opportunities, and the lack of a mutual support network. The Stephen Lawrence Trust programme had run for twelve years, providing 92 UK-based and 14 international bursaries. Evaluation and review were timely and important in order to assess the impact of what had been achieved, and to attract new donors for the programme.

Activities
TRIF supported activities included:

* undertaking a summative evaluation to decide how well funds had been spent
* e-mailing all students who had received bursaries from 2000 to 2010 with a questionnaire requesting information about career progression and responses to the Stephen Lawrence Trust programme
* collation and analysis of results to help identify lessons for the future of the programme

Section 1
Section 2
Section 3
Section 4
Section 5
Section 6
Section 7
Section 8

Case study 14 Stephen Lawrence Charitable Trust: Bursary and Alumni Programme evaluation. CONTINUED...

Impact

The evaluation highlighted the experience of Tendai Mutyasera, a bursary recipient, who said:

'The Stephen Lawrence Charitable Trust's philanthropy has taken me from the verge of dropping out of architectural study to work experience in America designing international airports to working for one of the largest architectural firms in the UK designing high-rise buildings. For me, the work of the Trust has been a life-changing experience that has catapulted me from the corridors of the Student Union to the corridors of Downing Street, to meeting princes, ambassadors, politicians and international architects ... a world apart from my humble beginnings. Now that I am a fully qualified architect, the future seems full of endless opportunities, an exhilarating optimism I've never known'.

Leading the way

The Stephen Lawrence Charitable Trust is leading the way because:

- it used qualitative evaluation to measure the progress of its work against its original aims
- it drew on the bursary recipients' first-hand experiences to decide whether what it was doing was sufficiently life-changing
- it used the evaluation outcomes to decide how best to take its work forward

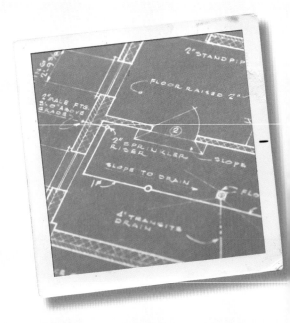

Case study 15
Peterborough Racial Equality Council: StepUp and 'ABC' focus group

The organisation

StepUp is a third sector organisation engaging disadvantaged communities in the East of England, in particular targeting young people and females in order to increase their self-reliance and participation in society. Peterborough Racial Equality Council and StepUp worked together on the ABC initiative.

The challenge

The aim was to bring together BAME young people into a focus group which could highlight inequalities within Peterborough and identify ways in which these might be tackled. The longer-term intention was that the forum should be well-established, active, recognised by key groups and services in Peterborough, and self-sufficient with its own independent funding. The group was named ABC, standing for: Assume nothing, Believe no-one, Challenge everything.

Activities
As its TRIF supported activity StepUp:

- held workshops for focus group members using role play, improvisation and discussion to cover such areas as identity, culture, inequalities, aspirations and expectations
- introduced key speakers who spoke of their own experiences of inequality or described their own organisation's work
- took the ABC group for a residential trip to London to consider aspirational role models and to be introduced to TAGMAP, a social networking site for young people to talk about social issues
- identified three areas where BAME young people were most likely to experience discrimination: education, police, media/communications sector

Impact
Impact included:

- a group of empowered BAME young people able to identify and speak out against racial and other inequalities
- year 1 outcomes which can be used to develop anti-discriminatory strategies by the group, including working with other organisations and helping other young people to speak out against inequality

Section 1
Section 2
Section 3
Section 4
Section 5
Section 6
Section 7
Section 8

Case study 15 Peterborough Racial Equality Council: StepUp and 'ABC' focus group. CONTINUED...

The young people say:

'The project has really helped me understand that a lot of other people are going through the same problems as me and my friends go through ... Being part of the forum, I have become more confident to speak out against racism ... I want to help other young people challenge the inequalities because when I was younger, we had no-one to help us'
Hussnain, aged 19 years

'The ABC forum has empowered me to really make a difference. I know I have to challenge people's attitudes and will not hesitate to speak up for others ... We all know it will take many years for things to be fully equal but if we all stand up and speak out against racial inequalities, this will definitely lead to major changes'.
Jav, aged 22 years

'Without this forum racial equalities faced by BAME young people would never had been highlighted ... the support has allowed like-minded individuals to come together and look at ways of tackling race issues ... We also talked to the police and schools and made them accountable for their actions with BAME young people'.
Tiago, aged 19 years

Leading the way
StepUp is leading the way because:

- ABC uses the direct experiences of BAME young people to hold services to account
- StepUp provided the right training to enable young people to understand the issues
- ABC will progress beyond identifying the issues to deciding how they can be tackled

The initiative was supported by MENTER – the East of England Black and Minority Ethnic Network which supported five TRIF projects.

Case study 16

Bedford African Community Support Project: Africa Beats Club Youth Forum

The organisation

Bedford African Community Support Project (BACSP) supports Africans living in Bedford. It provides a range of services, including welfare and benefits information, employment guidance, IT skills, translation services and English classes, and referral to other services. BACSP worked with Africa Beats Club for its TRIF activity.

The challenge

The challenge for BACSP was to engage with African young people in order to explore racial inequalities in Bedford and to tackle gaps in services. In order to set up the Youth Forum it worked with Africa Beats Club which had well-established contact with these young people.

Activities

Activities included:

- presentations, debates and guest speakers including police representatives
- history workshops
- community volunteering
- mentor training
- workshops on identity and presentation

Impact

Impact for Obed, one of the Youth Forum members included:

- developing self-confidence and skills through initiating and organising meetings
- joining the Independent Advisory Group of the local Police Authority where he is the youngest member
- acting as mentor to two other African young people
- volunteering for an organisation tackling race discrimination

Leading the way

Bedford African Community Support Project is leading the way because it:

- chose the right partner to reach the group it had in mind
- used TRIF support to work with a specific group of young people

- does not see the Forum as a 'one off' but intends to continue the partnership work with Africa Beats Club, and is actively seeking funds for a second year

The initiative was supported by MENTER – the East of England Black and Minority Ethnic Network which supported five TRIF projects.

Case study 17

Chara Trust: developing BAME volunteers and staff

The organisation

Chara Trust is a Black-led charity based in Liverpool, which offers capacity building, personal development and support to representative organisations and individuals from disadvantaged communities across Merseyside and the North West. For its first five years, the Trust was run by volunteers. It is a member of the NBP.

The challenge

Chara Trust aims to unlock the potential in individuals, organisations and communities by deploying the skills and experiences of its highly-motivated staff, most of whom began as volunteers.

Activities

Chara Trust's TRIF activities include:

- the Merseyside BAME Legacy Project which helps ensure the BAME voluntary sector on Merseyside has access to the best support services
- neighbourhood-based learning programmes
- capacity building with BAME and disadvantaged groups
- Steps to Employability programme aimed at BAME unemployed people

Impact

Impact included:

- some 250 individuals and 50 voluntary groups benefiting each year
- over 30 Chara Trust volunteers progressing to employment, training or other opportunities
- representation on local and regional education and community engagement groups
- strong reputation and high quality service recognised in recent inspection report

Leading the way

Chara Trust is leading the way because:

- it demonstrates that BAME volunteers can lead a grass-roots organisation into a professional set-up with a high reputation
- it has clear aims and objectives and a strong team approach with a powerful sense of community and commitment
- it views its grass-roots origins as a strength, coupled with the right strategic positioning

ARC: BME Training for All

The organisation

ARC is a well-established national organisation supporting providers of services for people with learning disabilities.

The challenge

Many third sector BAME organisations providing social care for people with learning disabilities often have limited access to culturally appropriate training. This limitation impacts on their ability to provide the right services to their clients. In addition, people from BAME communities are under-represented in the social care workforce.

Activities
As part of its TRIF activities, ARC:

- set up the Training for All project overseen by an advisory group representing statutory bodies, sector skills councils, education, social care and others

- developed a set of protocols for training developers and providers aimed at improving access to training which is culturally appropriate

- made these protocols available on the internet

Impact
Impact included:

- UK organisations working with BAME people with learning disabilities and/or seeking to increase BAME representation in their staff now able to access practical protocols which improve training

- increased awareness amongst project participants of the service needs of BAME people with learning disabilities

Leading the way
ARC is leading the way because:

- it understands that BAME social care providers require tailored training

- it knows that if more organisations had more BAME staff then more BAME clients would get a better deal

- it is providing practical help to BAME organisations, developed by practitioners

Section 6

Section 1

Section 2

Section 3

Section 4

Section 5

Section 6

Section 7

Section 8

Case study 19

Friends, Families and Travellers: strengthening the voice of Gypsy and Travelling groups

The organisation

Friends, Families and Travellers is a national organisation working on behalf of all Gypsies and Travellers. It combines service delivery with strategic and policy work.

The challenge

Gypsies and Travellers have very little involvement in the decisions which affect their lives. Some grass-roots groups fail because members do not understand governance and accountability issues, or because they cannot secure funding. Although some statutory authorities engage Travelling communities in regular Travellers Forum meetings, there are large parts of the country where no opportunities exist for communities to have their say and to influence decisions.

Activities

As part of its TRIF work, Friends, Families and Travellers helped to develop the capacity of twelve Gypsy/Traveller groups; activities in the South-East included:

- setting up a residents group on a local authority Gypsy site, so that residents meet quarterly with local councillors, site managers, the Traveller education service, police and fire-service to discuss installing site showers and lighting, rubbish collection, and potential relocation to another site

- encouraging Gypsies and Travellers to register on electoral rolls thereby increasing their involvement in democratic processes, and working with a local authority to pilot innovative ways of increasing Traveller engagement

- brokering mediation training for Gypsies and Travellers provided by six specialist agencies, with training for mediation volunteers from the communities

- linking the TRIF work to a Department of Health project aimed at improving Gypsy and Traveller access to the NHS

Overall, the organisation supported twelve grass-roots organisations in three regions.

Impact

Impact included:

- increased capacity to engage in the democratic process and to articulate their needs by previously unorganised Gypsy and Traveller groups

- strengthened relationships with local authorities which are now more aware of the communities' needs and know how best to meet them

- communities with better strategies for conflict resolution thereby lessening internal conflict and conflict with the settled community

- mediation volunteers able to build on their new-found skills and confidence in order to take part in other training opportunities

- successful approaches which can be replicated in other areas of the country

Leading the way

Friends, Families and Travellers is leading the way because:

- it works directly to build the capacity of grass-roots groups which might fail without expert support

- it identified gaps in services such as in the spread of local authority Travellers Forums, and worked to fill them

- it uses the lessons learnt in one area of work to enhance work in another area

Section 6

Case study 20

Greater Merseyside Learning Providers Federation: recruiting and supporting BAME staff

The organisation

Greater Merseyside Learning Providers Federation is a not-for-profit organisation representing work-based learning providers in Merseyside. It has 54 members across six boroughs and supports borough networks to improve provision, share best practice and to consider strategic issues.

The challenge

The challenge for Greater Merseyside Learning Providers Federation was to recruit and successfully support an Apprentice from the BAME community in Toxteth, one of the most deprived areas of Liverpool.

Activities

As part of its TRIF activities, the Federation:

- recruited Amanda as an Apprentice in Business Administration, liaising with Training Plus Merseyside for the Apprenticeship programme delivery

- promoted her to full-time employment as Administrative Assistant

- supported her to successful completion of her Apprenticeship within a year

- assisted her to apply for a Level 3 Advanced Apprenticeship, and supported her completion, again within a year

- ensured Amanda had substantial projects to run, including data management for the Network's Capital of Culture apprenticeship programme, and supporting the Network's training programmes

- helped Amanda increase her self-confidence by, for example, supporting her in taking over the front page of the local newspaper for a day as part of the Capital of Culture programme, by arranging that she receive her First Aid certificate from the former Leader of Liverpool City Council, and by putting her forward successfully to represent the BAME community in Connexions publicity material

- supported Amanda's ambition by enabling her to visit Edge Hill University to discuss taking a BA in Business Administration

Impact

Impact has included:

- a young BAME person fulfilling her potential and with ambitious plans for the future

- an organisation able to make use of the skills and understanding of a young BAME person with a similar background to many of the learners with whom the Federation member providers work

- increased BAME representation within the Federation which has also increased the number of BAME learners on its Accelerated Programme Led Pathway programme which prepares young people for Apprenticeships

Leading the way

Greater Merseyside Learning Providers Federation is leading the way because:

- it is working actively to recruit from its local BAME community, and understands the business benefits of having BAME staff

- it provided support and a career pathway for the BAME Apprentice so she could achieve her potential

- it has achieved Grade 1 for learner progression and learner support in its Ofsted inspection

- it has secured Investors in People and maintains the Skills Pledge as part of its commitment to developing all its staff

Section 6

Section 1

Section 2

Section 3

Section 4

Section 5

Section 6

Section 7

Section 8

Leading the way: personal testimonies

Organisations lead the way to equality, but so do individuals within them. As part of its TRIF work, the NBP commissioned Race Inequalities and Positive Action, the report described early on in this Guide. An important part of the report is a series of personal testimonies that illuminate the experiences of BAME people leading the way to equality. Three of these testimonials follow in shortened form along with suggestions to help think about what the testimonials tell us.

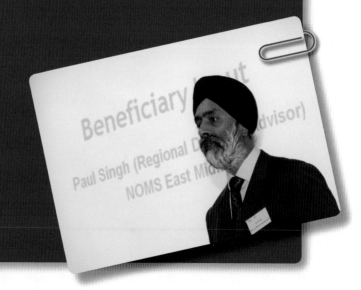

Beneficiary ...ut

Paul Singh (Regional D...   ...dvisor)

NOMS East Mid...

Case study 21
'Getting back the inner belief in myself'

Simon (not his actual name) came to Britain from Jamaica when he was seven. He was the first Black boy in his local grammar school. Eventually he became assistant head boy but he feels this was mainly because of his sports prowess. He feels the education system did not serve him well because he was pushed into sports at school rather than being encouraged to develop academically. He became an apprentice with a local football club but considers with hindsight, that this was not a positive move. He did not have the opportunity to take A-levels and go to university.

After working in sports and recreation for a few years, he secured a permanent job in a public training institution and progressed to middle management where he remained for twelve years. He felt there was a lack of opportunity for progression, and whilst there were no obvious issues or conflict with colleagues or employer, he was frustrated at not being able to progress to a more senior position and higher salary. He saw other people moving up while he remained stuck. He knew he was considered to be very good at operational level; there was no incentive for the organisation to promote him because he was valuable where he was.

Simon began to lose confidence in himself. He says: 'I had become like a novice, a beginner in the job market. I was no longer sure what HR people were looking for when they made selection decisions. I used to think I had to meet all the requirements of a job before applying, but I was perplexed to see White people with far less experience just going for jobs and getting them'. Simon became desperate enough to consider a complete career change.

The turning point came when Simon met someone from the NBP who persuaded him to go onto its First Steps to Leadership programme. The BLI® mentoring and support changed everything, 'Someone from outside my day-to-day work life was telling me I can do what I want to do; they helped me break down the mental blocks that had built up, and helped me to regain an inner belief once more'.

Simon is now in a strategic education post in a City Council. He is sure he would not have applied for the post without the Network's support. Simon feels that he has been a trail-blazer in each of his work environments because he has always been the most senior Black person there, with no-one like him to talk to or to share experiences with. Simon feels that the loss of confidence he experienced as a result of not progressing at work coupled with not wishing to be labelled as having a chip on his shoulder, played a big part in his not articulating or achieving what he wanted to do. It took outside help for him to regain his belief in his capability.

Case study 22
'I felt really valued for the first time in my work-life'

Jannett worked in the private sector after graduating and then started to teach in further education after her second child was born. She felt she would be able to manage her work and childcare responsibilities more flexibly. The public sector was very different from the private sector, and she experienced something of a culture shock when she heard about equalities policies, trades unions, and progression based supposedly on meritocracy.

Jannett saw an advert for the First Steps to Leadership programme and despite having no strong views about positive action at the time, decided to follow it up. Until then, she had not thought much about inequality but had questioned why she could see so few BAME people in leadership positions in further education. She says, 'I used to think my Black peers are very talented people, so why is this happening?' Importantly for her, the First Steps programme was free.

Her decision proved to be a turning-point in her career. 'I loved it.

I felt really valued for the first time in my working life, and privileged to be on a programme with such talented Black staff, including college principals. It was my first exposure to policy issues, and I heard about how to be a better manager from people outside my own college. I could also compare my own college with others'.

Jannett was assigned a mentor who was also a mother and understood her desire to help her maintain a good work/life balance.

Jannett says that though BAME teachers can be good in the classroom, transition to leadership and management can be very difficult, as many do not see any opportunities within their own further education colleges. She believes BAME people undersell themselves either through lack of confidence or because they think their skills and knowledge will be considered irrelevant. The First Steps programme provided strategies for breaking into leadership roles. Her self-belief strengthened by the programme, Jannett took on some consulting work outside her college.

Jannett then became a manager in the NBP. The Network helps people develop beyond qualifications and skills that are needed to take on promotion and leadership roles. Jannett recognises there is still a lot to do, especially when 'some people think of positive action as a dirty word'. She is particularly concerned that race will slip off the agenda, with people thinking 'we have done race so now we'll move on to class'.

Jannett says that political commitment and leadership are key to race equality, but worries this may be lessening after the impetus provided by the Macpherson Report. Jannett is now an independent consultant.

'Where will future BAME leaders come from?'

Jeremy left school without qualifications, but became involved early on with the third sector partly because his mother was a community worker. Eventually, he went back into education and met older male teachers who took him seriously and helped increase his confidence. He says, 'Just having conversations about education can help you. Coming from an older man can make a big difference'.

His first paid job in the voluntary sector did not work out well but allowed him to learn a lot. Jeremy worked his way up to management posts in the sector, and is now the director of an established voluntary organisation. He says that he has taken a roundabout route to get there, 'I never had a career plan to be a director. I grasped opportunities where I could, and then used my skills in the jobs I had. Most of my development has been informal, though I have been on Common Purpose and other programmes where you meet senior people from other settings'.

Jeremy had the opportunity to learn about how to work with senior civil servants and ministers when he took up a secondment in a government department. He also sat on partnership boards with other successful CEOs and could learn from them, as well as noticing the high level of respect he was accorded by them. He views all these activities as valuable opportunities to learn from other people and to find out more about the process of policy development.

Jeremy thinks his success is down to his considerable determination together with a supportive Board, which understood the benefits to the organisation of allowing him to take time out for professional development. He feels BAME third sector organisations face particular challenges when it comes to developing new leaders, and says, 'Most people think of charities as being White organisations. Few BAME people are included in lists of role models for young people. It's a real problem. How are BAME future leaders going to be attracted into the third sector, and where will they come from?'

Jeremy is deeply committed to help other talented BAME people to progress in the sector. He is proud that many of his own organisation's staff have progressed to more senior jobs. He says, 'We don't fear people with better specific skills or knowledge... we are about policy issues – not personalities. That's the important thing'.

Section 6

Section 1

Section 2

Section 3

Section 4

Section 5

Section 6

Section 7

Section 8

What do the testimonials tell us?

The three testimonials tell us important things about how best to develop and nurture BAME staff in order to unlock their potential as leaders in effective intercultural organisations. These things include:

- the importance of valuing staff by treating their different skills and experiences with respect

- the need for policies, structures, processes and practices which nurture BAME talent and enable talented, ambitious BAME staff to become leaders

- recognising that the right professional development can act as a turning-point for BAME staff, and ensuring these opportunities exist

- the importance of BAME mentors and role models from whom people can learn and receive support

- the power of self-belief which, with the right opportunities and support, can transform a person's life and help change the organisation they work in

The case studies and testimonials provide powerful examples of organisations and individuals leading the way to race equality. In the last section of the Guide, we look at how this kind of progress can be sustained.

Section 7.
Keeping up momentum

The Department for Communities and Local Government's TRIF initiative made it possible for organisations to spread their wings, and do the things they knew needed doing but for which they did not have the resources. Because of the fund, organisations are better able to play their part in creating the fair society described by the Prime Minister. Their power stems from their first-hand understanding of the experiences, aspirations and strengths of BAME communities. It is striking how many of the featured projects involve self-advocacy, finding a voice, or sharing experiences as the first step to empowerment.

The next step, already taken by some projects, is to use that first-hand experience to help form regional or national policy. Making that jump can be a challenge for a small organisation. The answer is to work with other organisations and become 'more than the sum of the parts' by finding a shared agenda and unified voice. Oxfam's Routes to Solidarity project demonstrates the power of collaboration and a single voice, as well as the ways in which smaller organisations can be supported to work together at individual, local, and national levels.

As well as working together, organisations can benefit by using the approaches developed by the NBP through the BLI®. The idea of intercultural effectiveness, the National Occupational Standards for Intercultural Working, and the individual and organisational checklists are all valuable tools which strengthen any organisation's capacity to meet the needs of its BAME customers or service-users.

If the projects outlined in this Good Practice Guide are to continue to lead the way to race equality, then their outcomes and lessons need to be embedded in the organisations as part and parcel of their everyday work, not as 'one-off' activities.

Most of the TRIF partners plan to keep the work alive by finding new partners or new funding sources, or by changing the way they do things to include the approaches and lessons from the TRIF activities.

Actions to take

As part of its TRIF activities, the NBP has identified eight actions which organisations can take in order to continue to lead the way in race equality. They are:

1. Understand the demographic changes in the UK and what they mean for your business; people from BAME groups will become increasingly important as customers/service-users, and as part of the labour market.

2. Recognise the business imperative for equality in recruitment, access to promotion and to professional development; organisations with BAME representation at all levels are better able to meet the needs of BAME customers/service-users.

3. Ensure excellence, be at the top of your game by using the National Occupational approaches and practical help in this Guide; benchmark your organisation against others to find out where you stand in relation to race equality.

4. Assess your organisation's progress toward intercultural effectiveness, and action plan to improve; include recruiting strategies in your plan.

5. Collaborate with organisations which are interculturally competent so that they help your organisation achieve its strategic aims, and add to its expertise and skills.

6. Build your organisation's reputation; tell other people what you do well, share your good practice; excellence attracts excellence in the people wanting to work in your organisation, new partnerships, and funding opportunities.

7. Deploy the diverse skills and perspectives of all your staff; understand what your organisation can gain from the range of staff experience.

8. Unlock the potential of staff members, engage in Succession Planning which involves them, and encourage participation on BLI® programmes

In a truly fair society, each person must be able to lead a fulfilling and fulfilled life, able to articulate their legitimate needs and to have them met, and empowered to release their full potential. This Guide illustrates how organisations across England are working to make this vision a reality for Black, Asian and Minority Ethnic people.

Section 8.
Acknowledgements

Thanks to all the following people and publications, from whom invaluable help, guidance, time and effort has been gratefully offered. Without it this publication would not have been possible.

- **Robin Landman OBE.** Chief Executive Officer NBP
- **Rajinder Mann.** Executive Director NBP
- **Lenford White.** Regional Development Manager NBP
- **Pat Hood.** Editor
- Staff and participants of the twenty case studies (see opposite page)
- Providers of three personal testimonies for kind permission to use their stories

- **Frank Anti.** Head of Policy, Black Training & Enterprise Group (BTEG), 2nd Floor, Lancaster House, 31-33 Islington High Street, London, N1 9LH. T: 020 7843 6134 E: Frank@bteg.co.uk W: www.bteg.co.uk

- **Hughbon Condor.** PATH Manager, 29 Harrogate Rd, Chapel Allerton, Leeds, LS7 3PD T: 0113 2624 600 F: 0113 2374872 E: hughbon.condor@pathyorkshire.co.uk

- **Stan Pochron**. Chief Executive Officer, Greater Merseyside Learning Providers Federation, 2nd Floor Saunders House, Parliament Business Park, Commerce Way, L8 7BA T: 0151 707 8775 E: stan@gmlpf.net

- **Femi Sowande.** JET, South Central Dingle Office, 300 Park Road, Toxteth, Liverpool. L8 4UE. T: 0151 726 1634 F: 0151 726 0036 E: femis@dingle.net

- **Karen Bellion.** Liverpool - People First, People First Merseyside. MPAC Building, 1-27 Bridport Street Liverpool L3 5QF. T: 0151 707 6751 F: 0151 708 6480 E: karenbellion@yahoo.co.uk

- **Godwin Bateren.** CEO Chara Trust, 64 Upper Parliament Street, Liverpool, L8 7LF. T: 0151 708 5146 E: gbateren@yahoo.co.uk W: www.charatrust.org.uk

- **Chris Whitwell.** Director, Friends, Families and Travellers, Community Base, 113 Queens Road, Brighton, BN1 3XG. T: 01273 234 772 E: chris@gypsy-traveller.org

- **Race on the Agenda.** Unit 217, Waterloo Business Centre 117 Waterloo Road London SE1 8UL T: 020 7902 1177 F: 020 7921 0036 E: rota@rota.org.uk

- **Alison Chapman.** Production Co-ordinator, The Rural Media Company, Sullivan House 72-80, Widemarsh Street, Hereford, HR4 9HG. T: 01432 344 039 E: alisonc@ruralmedia.co.uk W: www.ruralmedia.co.uk

- **Farah Kurji.** Routes to Solidarity Project Officer. Oxfam UK. Poverty 1st floor, 494 Wilbraham Road, Chorlton, Manchester M21 9AS. T: 0161 861 7940 M: 0782 4334 167 E: fkurji@oxfam.org.uk

- **Katrina Roberts.** Ass. Project Manager Wirral Council S&I, Wallasey Town Hall, South Annex, Brighton St, CH44 8ED. T: 0151 691 8382 E: katrinaroberts@wirral.gov.uk

- **Daniel Silver.** One North West Coordinator, North West Network, 2nd Floor, Albert House, 17 Bloom Street, Manchester, M1 3HZ. T: 0161 236 6493 F: 0161 228 6137 E: danielsilver@nwnetwork.org.uk W: www.onenorthwest.org.uk W: www.nwnetwork.org.uk

- **Anna Burgess.** Regional Equalities Partnership Officer, Menter, 62-64 Victoria Road, Cambridge, CB4 3DU. T: 01223 35034 E: anna@menter.org.uk

- **Nathan Lewis.** Senior Administrator, The 1990 Trust, CAN Mezzanine, 49-51 East Road. Old Street, London N1 6AH. T: 0207 250 8066 E: nathan@1990trust.org.uk

- **Aledina Miah.** Community development and office co-ordinator, Olmec, 2 Bath Place, Rivington Street, London EC2A 3DR. T: 0207 749 5180 F: 0208 616 0511 M: 0797 2007 412 E: aledina.miah@olmec-ec.org.uk W: www.olmec-ec.org.uk

- **The Stephen Lawrence Charitable Trust.** The Stephen Lawrence Centre, 39 Brookmill Road, London, SE8 4HU. T: 020 8100 2800 E: information@stephenlawrence.org.uk

- **David Grundy Training for All Project Worker ARC.** ARC House, Marsden Street, Chesterfield, Derbyshire, S40 1JY. T: 01246 564970 F: 01246 564971 M: 07931 116099 E: david.grundy@arcuk.org.uk

Acronym Buster

1. **BAME** – Black, Asian and Minority Ethnic
2. **TRIF** – Tackling Race Inequalities Fund
3. **CLG** – Department for Communities and Local Government
4. **NBP** – Network for Black Professionals
5. **BLI®** – Black Leadership initiative
6. **JET** – Jobs Education and Training
7. **NAS** – National Apprenticeship Service
8. **BTEG** – Black Training and Enterprise Group
9. **DIUS** – Department of Innovation Universities and skills
10. **ROTA** – Race on The Agenda
11. **MENTER** – Minority Ethnic Network for the Eastern Regions
12. **FE** – Further Education
13. **CDWs** – Career Development Workshop
14. **GRT** – Gypsy, Roma and Travelling

Section 8

Sources of information and advice

- Asian Jobsite:
  www.asianjobsite.co.uk
- Black Information Link (BLINK):
  www.blink.org.uk
- Black Training and Enterprise Group (BTEG):
  www.bteg.co.uk
- British Institute for Human Rights:
  www.bihr.org.uk
- Business Link:
  www.businesslink.gov.uk
- The Diversity Group:
  www.thediversitygroup.co.uk
- Diversity Job site:
  www.diversityjobsite.co.uk
- Ethnic Minority Taskforce:
  www.emataskforce.gov.uk
- Equality and Diversity Forum:
  www.edf.org.uk
- Equality Britain:
  www.equalitybritain.co.uk
- Equality Challenge Unit:
  www.ecu.ac.uk
- Equality and Human Rights Commission:
  www.equalityhumanrights.com

- Equality Recruitment:
  www.equalityrecruitment.co.uk
- Hope not Hate:
  www.hopenothate.org.uk/tufs
- Institute for Race Relations:
  www.irr.org.uk
- Joseph Rowntree Foundation:
  www.jrf.org.uk
- The National Mentoring Consortium (NMC):
  www.uel.ac.uk/nmc/schemes/ethnic.htm
- The NBP:
  www.nbp.org.uk
- Operation Black Vote:
  http://obv.org.uk
- Race for Opportunity:
  www.bitc.org.uk/workplace
- Race on the Agenda:
  www.rota.org.uk
- Runnymede Trust:
  www.runnymedetrust.org
- Searchlight:
  www.searchlightmagazine.com
- Trade Union Congress (TUC):
  www.tuc.org.uk/equality/tuc-16205-f0.cfm

Useful reports and publications

- **How Fair is Britain? Equality and Human Rights Commission, 2010.**
  http://www.equalityhumanrights.com/key-projects/triennial-review/online-summary/

- **Tackling Race Inequality: A Statement on Race, Department for Communities and Local Government, January 2010.**
  http://www.communities.gov.uk/documents/communities/pdf/1432344.pdf

- **Impact of the Economic Downturn on Black and Minority Ethnic Third Sector Organisation, CEMVO, March 2010.**
  http://www.cemvo.org.uk/download%20files/CEMVO%20-%20Recession%20Report.pdf

- **Positive Action Briefing Note, Equality and Human Rights Commission, July 2009.**
  http://www.lawcentres.org.uk/uploads/EHRC_Positive_Action_Briefing.pdf

- **The Value of Difference: Eliminating Bias in Organisations, Kandola, 2009.**
  http://www.amazon.co.uk/Value-Difference-Eliminating-Bias-Organisations/dp/0956231802

- **The Economic Downturn and the Black, Asian and Minority Ethnic (BAME) third sector: ROTA, June 2009.**
  http://www.rota.org.uk/Downloads/Recession%20Report%20-%20ROTA%202009%20Ex%20Summary.pdf

- **Black, Asian and Minority Ethnic Leadership in the Creative and Cultural Sector, Cultural Leadership Programme 2009.**
  http://www.culturalleadership.org.uk/uploads/tx_rtgfiles/Black__Asian_and_Minority_Ethnic_Leadership.pdf

- **Transparency at the Heart of Diversity, Business in the Community, Benchmarking Report, RfO, 2009.**
  www.bitc.org.uk/document.rm?id=9563

- **The Experience of Black and Minority Ethnic Staff Working in Higher Education, Literature Review, ECU, 2009.**
  http://www.ecu.ac.uk/publications/files/experience-of-bme-staff-in-he.pdf/view?searchterm=Experiences of black and minority ethnic staff working in higher education: literature review 2009

- **Diversity in Higher Education: Leadership Responsibilities and Challenges, Leadership Foundation for Higher Education, D Bebbington, November 2009.**
  http://www.lfhe.ac.uk/publications/research.html

- **Equal Opportunities and Diversity for Staff in Higher Education: Negotiating Equity in Higher Education Institutions, Deem, Morley, Tlili. Higher Education Funding Council for England, 2005.**
  http://eprints.sussex.ac.uk/134/01/negotiating_equity.pdf

- **A Test for Racial Discrimination in Recruitment Practice in British Cities, Wood, Hales, Purdon, Sejersen, Hayllar, Research Report No 607, Department for Work and Pensions, October 2009.**
  http://www.admin.ox.ac.uk/eop/raceq/DWP.pdf

- **Race to the Top: The Place of Ethnic Minority Groups in the UK Workforce, Business in the Community, December 2008.**
  www.bitc.org.uk/document.rm?id=8676